The Transformation of Thomas Watson

A CHRIS Kid

This memoir is an inspirational story that reminds us that no one makes it without help and demonstrates that with the right help, even the most challenged kid can make it. Thankfully, Thomas has the courage to give us this insight into his struggle and triumph.

Andrew Young, Former Mayor of Atlanta

Thomas' story is a true testimony of hope for individuals that need support through our behavioral health system. I am touched by his story and the great strides he has accomplished in his life because recovery and independence are real. The Department of Behavioral Health and Developmental Disabilities believes that every person should live an independent life in the community. Thomas' perseverance, despite the many setbacks he faced, underscores the value of programs like CHRIS Kids. Thomas has a story of hope for those who have given up and reminds us of the infinite possibilities of community-based treatment. His story makes our work worth it.

Frank W. Berry, Commissioner, Georgia Department of Behavioral Health and Developmental Disabilities

The Transformation of Thomas Watson

A CHRIS Kid

Thomas Leon Watson

CHRIS Kids

CHRIS Kids

ISBN 978-1-304-13278-9

CREDITS

Illustrations and Front Cover Design

Katie Ridley
kridleyink@yahoo.com

Copyediting

Contributed by *The Toccoa Recor*
toccoarecord@windstream.net

Tom Law, Publisher
Duane H. Winn, Copy Editor

DEDICATION

In memory of my mother and father, Betty Arthur Watson and
Joshua Paris Hazard. Without you there would be no Thomas
Leon Watson.

Mom, I thank God for you daily. I remember the sacrifices that
you made for me and for Curtis. Thank you for being there for
me in all of my struggles, comforting me when I needed it most.
You always encouraged me to write down my feelings and
experiences, telling me that one day I would write a book. You
are my angel and thank you very much for the memories.

DEDICATION

Dad, I remember the day that we were separated and the pain that I felt in my heart. But my best moment was the day that we reconnected after twenty years. Getting to know you helped me become a better man. I thank God for the time that we spent together. Though it was cut short, you live forever in my heart.

Most importantly, I dedicate this book to my Heavenly Father who placed His Word inside of me through my life experiences. For this reason I cannot remain silent. He gave me my voice.

CONTENTS

PREFACE

I am touched, honored and proud to be asked to write this preface. Remembering the 17-year old boy, a football player with multiple psychiatric hospitalizations since he was 13, years of non-compliance with medications and a huge problem with anger, I reflect upon how far Thomas Leon Watson has come.

He called himself Leon when he was referred by his caseworker to CHRIS Kids. When I received the referral and reviewed his records, it was clear that Leon had many problems. But he also had a Mom who cared, so I invited her to come with Leon to the interview. At first, I talked with them together. Then, searching for chinks in the anger that cloaked him like armor, I spent time talking with just Leon. Like so many kids coming for interviews at CHRIS Kids, Leon was full of rage. He didn't understand anything about his mental health diagnosis or what it meant, and he didn't trust adults, especially men. He was aggressive, on the verge of going down a path that would likely lead to jail or death. Leon was 17 years old — which also meant that he thought he knew everything.

His Mom cared about him and he cared about her. That was a good place to start and there was something else — Leon was sensitive. And, he had goals. There *were* chinks in his armor. Leon would be a challenge, but I thought we could help him. After the interview Leon and his mom went back to Toccoa, Georgia. I asked Leon to think about what I told him about the expectations of our independent living program.

PREFACE

After talking with the staff at Georgia Mental Health Institute again, I called and let Leon know we would like for him to come to CHRIS Kids. He thought about it, then called back and said he was coming. That was our beginning. It was 1988.

Since 1981 CHRIS Kids had been helping kids ages 6 - 17 in foster care that had severe emotional and behavioral problems. The organization had opened an independent living program at the end of 1986 because when these kids turned 18, there was nothing available to help them make a successful transition to adulthood. I was hired as the director in September of 1987 and, at that time, I interviewed kids about coming into our programs. It wasn't long after his interview that Thomas Leon Watson joined the CHRIS Kids family.

During the next two years, there were many challenges and many talks. There were "conditions of continued placement" such as regular therapy. But together we stayed the course, stubbornly not giving up; knowing that progress is a journey with many twists and turns; understanding that sometimes you have to go back, to go forward; and sometimes you have to go down, to go up. Others may have given up, but CHRIS Kids doesn't and it paid off.

We felt pretty good about Leon when he decided to take the next step and leave CHRIS Kids. He had made tremendous progress and importantly, he seemed to understand that it was necessary for him to continue therapy and take his medication. His departure was bittersweet, but isn't it always like that when your children leave? Leon was now a member of the CHRIS Kids extended family — our child too. But like so many kids, he didn't keep in touch after he left.

Then many years later, the phone rang in my office. I was working on something and almost didn't pick up the call. A little voice in my head (to which I now pay close attention) said maybe you should pick up the phone, so I did. I recognized the voice on the other end, but could not place it. "Miss Kathy, this is Thomas. It's been 15 years since I was at CHRIS Kids and I thought I'd call you." I thought who is this? I know him. I know that voice. Then he said, "It's me, Leon. You knew me as Leon — Thomas Leon Watson. I am Thomas now."

Instantly it all came back to me. I almost fell out of my chair. Tears welled up in my eyes. So many times I had wondered about him, hoped he was doing OK. Overwhelmed with joy, I listened as he gave me a quick update on his life — married, working, with a church home. He explained that he goes by his first name now, Thomas. The name change must represent something about transformation because many former CHRIS kids who have contacted me over the years also make the decision to go by their other given name once they become adults. Thomas and I got together for lunch and now we are on another kind of journey together — a journey to give back. Today, Thomas is not my "kid," he is my friend.

This is Thomas' story, his journey to the present. I couldn't be more proud of Thomas, of the courage it took for him to write this book and of his commitment to giving back to help kids like him. While CHRIS Kids never gave up on Thomas and we provided the combination of acceptance, safety, stability, guidance, housing, accountability, support and therapy that made a huge difference, it was Thomas who made all the choices.

Thomas made the choice to come to CHRIS Kids and do what it took. Thomas had the courage to face and work through his anger and his fears. He had the willingness to learn. Thomas chose to face and accept what living with bi-polar disorder means. Then with this understanding, Thomas chose to commit to taking his medication.

PREFACE

Thomas chooses a spiritual path and to live his life in accordance with his values. Thomas chooses to accept himself and other people for who they are. Thomas chooses to practice forgiveness and in the process he found, and continues to find, his own healing. Today, Thomas strives to make positive, thoughtful choices. It is a joy, a privilege and an honor to have Thomas serve on the CHRIS Kids Board of Directors and for him to be one of my "bosses."

Good outcomes don't surprise me. I expect them. I believe in the resilience of the human spirit. I believe that if we provide our children with safety, love, individualized support, the array of services that they need and we help them face the truth of their situations, even the most damaged, troubled kids can succeed.

But I can honestly say that I never expected that today I would have the honor of working alongside the scared, angry young man that I interviewed in 1988. Today Thomas helps CHRIS

PREFACE

Kids unlock the potential of more than 2,000 children, youth and families each year through our integrated Family of Services: Behavioral Health, Safe Homes and Environments, Strong Communities and Education and Training. Today the program Thomas was in is called TransitionZ and our EarthCraft certified Summit Trail Apartment complex provides a safe, supportive environment for single and parenting homeless youth and youth aging out of foster care, ages 17 - 24, to help them become productive and self sufficient.

Thomas has the courage to tell his story. I hope that it inspires you. CHRIS Kids was able to stand in the gap for Thomas because everyday people made it possible through their support of the CHRIS Kids mission to heal children, strengthen families and build community. There are kids like Thomas in every community. Kids with potential. Kids who need someone to take the time to help them understand their situation, discover their strengths and talents, and help them heal wounds of abuse and abandonment so that they can become productive.

It is time to take action, to give of your energy, your talent and your resources. Together, we can ensure that kids, like Thomas, have the support, encouragement and opportunity they so richly deserve to enable them to make the choices that will help them reach their goals.

They can succeed when we all help.

Kathy Colbenson, LMFT

CEO, CHRIS Kids

INTRODUCTION

It has not been an easy task writing a book about my life story. At the age of thirteen I started keeping a journal of my life to record my feelings and life experiences. It was like an inner voice telling me to write so that I would not forget. Now, I would like to introduce you to the life of Thomas Leon Watson. I'm going to take you on the journey about my life, from childhood to adulthood.

This story is about a kid that was raised by a single mom that loved both of her kids. I was separated from my father at the age of three years old. Though I knew who my father was, I never got the chance to have a father and son relationship. This left a hole in my heart that could only be repaired by my real father or by anyone who wanted to fill his shoes. There were many attempts by lots of men trying to fill those shoes. And each failed attempt brought more feelings of abandonment. Abandonment eventually turned to anger, bitterness, hatred and resentment.

These feelings led to unpredictable behavior, which had unending consequences. I was institutionalized many times as an adolescent and diagnosed with a bi-polar disorder. I had to take medication. Since I did not understand the importance of taking medication at an early age, I found myself in and out of a mental hospital.

It became a vicious cycle. Then, I was introduced to an organization that helped change the course of my life. Here I began to get in touch with the reason why I was so angry and out

INTRODUCTION

of control. Slowly I began to heal. I was able to cultivate meaningful relationships and grew from being Leon, the little boy who experienced abandonment and was filled with anger, hatred, bitterness and rage into Thomas, a forty-four year old transformed man.

Each of us has a story to tell. As you read my book, I invite you to think about your own life and the things that you have overcome and the things you too may want to change. And finally, I hope that my story empowers you to renew your life.

Best wishes to you on *your* journey!

Thomas Leon Watson

CHAPTER 1

Childhood: 1 to 12

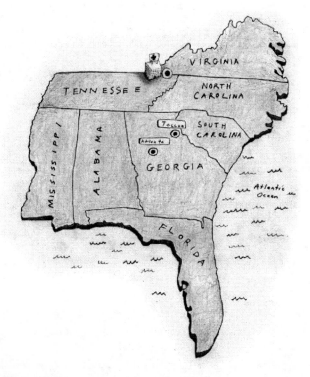

I was born Thomas Leon Watson on August 29, 1969, at Bristol Memorial Hospital in Tennessee. The hospital was built on the state line between Tennessee and Virginia. When my mother gave birth to me she lay on the bed in Virginia, but my head came out on the Tennessee side. That's the beginning of my story, my journey.

My mother was Betty Arthur Watson. I have one brother and we are a year apart. My mother was divorced from my brother's father and was never married to my father, JP. I remember at the age of four years old my mother decided to move from Virginia to Georgia. My father was there with some friends helping to load our belongings on the moving truck. My mother was saying goodbye to family members, so family started saying goodbye to my brother and me.

All of a sudden my father started saying goodbye to me. He picked me up and gave me a big hug and a kiss. I wondered, "Why is he saying goodbye?" When he set me back down, I grabbed his leg and tried to hold on forever. I didn't want to let go. I started crying because I didn't understand. I could only think, "Why is my father was not going with us?" After all, he was my dad. I got in the truck with my mother and brother. The truck took off.

I cried all the way from Virginia to Georgia. This was the first of many times that I would feel abandoned. After I stopped crying, I asked my mother, "Why didn't JP come with us?" All I remember her saying is, "I'm your mother *and* your father now." As a four-year old kid what could I say or do but cry, because I wanted my father to be with me. I wanted my dad to be there to throw the football, shoot basketball, hit the baseball with me, and just teach me how to be a boy.

We arrived in Toccoa, Georgia, where we lived with relatives for a little while. Then we moved into our own place across town in the projects. There were three sections to the projects and they were called Ridgecrest, Circle View and Brasswell. Each part of the projects was named after the street it was on. As a youngster

I lived on the Ridgecrest side and later, when I was a teenager, we moved to the Brasswell side. The projects were low-income public housing and that was our home. There were apartment units with a lot of kids. We had playgrounds and an outside basketball court surrounded by dirt and plenty of grass.

I remember my first day moving in. I met a guy who became my best friend. His name is Jermel Dortch and we are still best friends today. He was the only kid in the projects who had both a mother and father living with him. He also had two older brothers who were like big brothers to my brother and me. Everyone who lived in the projects was pretty close to one another. We treated each other like family.

After several months of settling into our apartment, Mom introduced us to her boyfriend whom we will call Mr. JD. He seemed cool. He was a tall man and his height reminded me of my dad. The more he spent time around my mom and us, the more comfortable everyone became, including me. In my mind, I was thinking, "Maybe Mr. JD can become my dad. Someone who will throw the football, shoot basketball, throw the baseball with me and be around for the rest of my life." When he came to the house to see my mom, he would always stop to play with me. He would pick me up and throw me in the air and let me go. Then he would catch me. I began to trust him, to know that each time he threw me up in the air he would catch me.

Then Mr. JD moved into our apartment with us. It was my mother, Mr. JD, my brother and me. After he moved in we saw more of him. All I know is that my mom was happy. I don't remember how my brother reacted. Mr. JD started playing catch with us in the yard. This was everything I thought a father is supposed to do with his son — have fun all the time. I allowed him to take the place of my father. He was the only father figure in my life.

In my mind, Mr. JD was my father. Then a year later, he picked me up, sat me on the countertop and said, "Son, there's something that I have to tell you. Me and your mother are breaking up. What this means is we are going our separate ways." He said, "I'm leaving your mother." As he turned his back to me and was leaving the apartment, I remember grabbing his leg and asking, "Why are you leaving?" He picked me up and tears were flowing down my eyes. I knew that this would be the last time that he picked me up and this time he wasn't going to throw me in the air and catch me. All the playing with Little Leon was about to walk out the door.

There was nothing that a five year old could do about it, except watch and cry. Yes, I felt disappointed, let down and sad. But guess what? I was five years old. I wasn't supposed to have feelings. I can only imagine now how my mother felt when her relationship with Mr. JD didn't work out. As an adult she was expected to feel emotions. But me? Not a five-year-old kid.

I brushed my feelings and emotions under the rug as if they never existed and went back to being a kid, which I enjoyed. I went back to playing with my brother and friends in the neighborhood. Riding my bike, playing hide and go seek, playing football and everything else kids do. It's amazing how quickly kids forget what happened just five minutes ago. Or, do kids really ever forget? I did go back to playing with my friends and I forgot all about the pain of leaving my father behind and now Mr. JD walking out on us. But the emotional wounds were there, hidden and buried — denied.

This is just the beginning of what grew into childhood and teenage anger, and almost led me to murdering a person when I was twelve years old. This anger also led me to five psychiatric hospital stays before I was eighteen years old. What saved me from a life behind prison bars, being institutionalized for life or trapped in my own mind? The next chapters in the story tell the tale of my recovery. At this point you may want to read this book or not. If you choose to continue and you can relate to my story or know others who may, please read on and inspire them to read it too.

After Mr. JD left I felt fatherless, but I didn't let it matter much because I returned to my friends. No other kids in the projects had a father in their homes either, except for my best friend. His two older brothers would teach all the kids how to play football. So, by the age of six I was playing little league football and my friend's brothers were my mentors for football. During all the pain, disappointments and anger that I experienced throughout childhood and my teenage years, my outlet was always football.

In grade school I was a good student, but I had a lot of conduct issues. Once I reached the fourth grade, I had all F's in conduct. I had an attitude problem. Really, it was an anger problem. I was always getting into fights and causing trouble. One time my best friend and I were hanging out in the schoolyard and another kid called us a bad name. I picked up a rock and threw it at the kid, hitting him in the head. Blood went everywhere and I was in big trouble. My friend was too.

One day I came home from school and my mother introduced us to Mr. E. I was respectful. I said, "Hello, Mr. E." This was my mother's second boyfriend. They dated for a while. Then he moved into the apartment with us. At the age of eight I was still hoping for someone who would be my father. I was happy to give him the chance to fill those shoes. He did things for us, took us out for ice cream, bought us things.

But the relationship between my mother and Mr. E didn't last. Later, he would have a talk with my brother and me. He said that he and my mother were breaking up. Once again, I was sad, disappointed and angry.

All I remember is stuffing my feelings and emotions inside and returning to my brother and friends, never telling anyone what was going on with me. No one knew how I felt.

I went on with my life. But things at school were getting worse. I pulled down the fire alarm in school, causing the buildings to be evacuated. I ran away from school after a teacher supposedly struck me on the arm. I was always in the principal's office being disciplined. Then when I got home, I got my butt whooped. Mom was very big on discipline with us. But by this time I was good at stuffing my feelings. I was just an angry child, heading out of control.

About two years passed without my mother having a live-in boyfriend. Then when I was ten, I was introduced to Mr. JW. When I first met him, he was different than the other men. He seemed to really like my mother a lot and he took a genuine interest in my brother and me. He played football, basketball and baseball with us. He helped me with my schoolwork.

Afterwards, when he moved in with us, he would cook, clean and sing. He was just a happy guy. He was more of a father figure to me than anyone. Everyone in the neighborhood liked him too. I remember things were going so well with my mother and him that they were talking about marriage.

But Mr. JW had a secret and it finally came out. He had another mistress living in the same neighborhood. This led to the break-up between my mother and Mr. JW. And it really hurt because I thought he would be there for us. I felt betrayed. Of all the male figures I had met, I believed that Mr. JW would become my mother's husband and the father to my brother and me.

The break-up did something to me. I was sad, disappointed, angry, and I felt let down, once again. But this time, something different happened. My heart turned hard and cold toward all men. I didn't trust them. I literally hated men. Yes, I looked at myself in the mirror daily and saw a man. But luckily I didn't grow up hating myself. My mom validated me daily. She told me how great I was and built up my self-esteem. She assured me, so I had good dose of love for myself.

But I still started to hate men. I made a decision that Mr. JW would be the last man that would ever come into my home and rule. I said to myself, "I will be the King of my home. I will protect it." I made a decision right then that some day I would reunite with my biological father. But for now, I didn't want a father if this is the way they are — always leaving. So, I placed a wall between men and me. A cold, hard wall.

My mom had a total of nine live-in boyfriends up until I graduated from high school, including Mr. RB, Mr. DL, Mr. NC, Mr. BH, Mr. CW, Mr. FG. I know what you are thinking about my mom. No, she was just trying to find love. From the many talks that I had with my mother, she was trying to fill the empty void in her heart. She told me she was looking for love.

In my eyes Betty Watson was a great mother. She was a beautiful, strong black woman. She was a single mom of two black boys. Mom worked hard to provide for us. I remember she used to wake up at four in the morning, cook us breakfast, then leave to walk to work. She would walk over twenty miles to get to the nursing home where she worked all day. Then she would walk home. She walked to every job she had, because we didn't have a car. She worked hard to make sure that we had food on the table, clothes on our backs and anything else that we needed. Though we grew up in the projects, mom made sure that we had everything that we needed. She loved us deeply and showed it in many, many ways. She just never could find the love she sought.

CHAPTER 2

Middle school, girls, the Bubble Gum Gang

"Lookin for the Perfect Beat"

I remember getting through elementary school and starting

middle school. I was very excited. I had to make a decision

whether I was going to play middle school football or continue to play recreation league football. The school was far away from our house and since we didn't have a car, I chose to play recreation league football. Playing football taught me how to work with other kids my age, learn teamwork and discipline.

I started playing football at the age of six. My best friend and his older brothers introduced me to the sport and I fell in love with it. It was a major outlet for me. I could be as aggressive as I wanted to be. I enjoyed playing defense because I liked hitting people. The anger that I had on the inside seemed to come out on the field in a good way. I also enjoyed having my family and friends watch me play.

When I wasn't playing football, you could find me hanging with two other close friends, Mark and Connery. Back in the early '80s, the thing to do was dance. Mark and Connery could dance! They used to always practice together. I remember one day they asked me if I could dance and I told them no. In my mind, all I could do was play football and that would be my ticket out of the projects. But the more I was around these guys the more I wanted to dance. It was hard for me to learn how to dance. Since my brother was a disc jockey and played his music 24/7, I started practicing at home. I would lock myself in my room for hours trying to tick and wave.

One night Mark and Connery were out dancing and I told them that I had learned a few dance moves. I showed them what I had. They played my favorite song, *Looking for the Perfect Beat*. When the song came on, I started popping, locking and ticking. They liked what they saw and the next thing you know I was practicing with them. We went to school, came home, walked across town to play basketball, then we came back home to practice dancing.

We began to dress alike, going to school and hanging tight. We started dancing some at school in the halls between breaks and on our lunches. We called ourselves the Bubble Gum Gang. Then other dancing groups began to form at school, across town and in the projects. This is the way that we used to fight—by dancing against each other.

I remember the first time that we danced together before a large crowd. It was at our middle school dance. There had been a lot of talk going on that other dance groups wanted to challenge us. We were pumped, ready for whatever was going to go down. Of course, the three of us had our dates. Sometime during the evening while I was with my date Mark found me and said, "Leon it's time to battle." Meaning another group challenged us to dance. I remember leaving my date and running to join my crew. We battled against these other dancing groups and won. To celebrate our victory, we threw bubble gum into the crowd and they loved it. That night people were introduced to the Bubble Gum Gang.

We kept practicing as a group. We danced together at the skating rink, at school, parks and clubs. One time we even entered a talent show contest and won first place. My brother was the DJ at the skating rink, so we had an in there. On Friday's during all night skating, the manager of the skating rink would pay us to dance at midnight. Everyone would gather around the skating rink floor and we would come out dressed alike and perform our dance routine. Wherever we performed the crowds loved us and we enjoyed giving them our best. And, most of all, we liked getting paid at the end.

During the time that we danced at the skating rink, I started liking girls. People were coming to our skating rink on Friday or Sunday just to see us dance. The girls loved us and I started loving them. There was this one girl that stood out. Her name was Kimberly. She was from a nearby city. She had come to watch us dance. After we danced, she introduced herself to me. Then we started a long distance relationship over the phone. We would meet at the skating rink every week, whether I was dancing or not. One night when we were about to depart she asked me to come over and she kissed me. This was my first real kiss. We dated each other for a couple of years.

Then I met another young lady named Abby. She would spend the summer with her grandmother who lived right in back of us. I remember the first time I saw her and her sister sitting in the yard. I went up and introduced myself. I used to look forward to seeing her each summer. We sat around talking and holding hands until her grandmother would call her into the house.

One day I was walking home and I saw Abby kissing on another guy. As I got closer, I realized it wasn't just another guy. It was one of my best friends, one of my dancing partners. This was the last time that I would speak to Abby or even see her. And it was a while before my friend and I would speak. Eventually we started hanging out again and being friends. I thought to myself,

"There are other girls." But for some time I calmed down on the girl scene and just focused on sports. Mainly football.

CHAPTER 3

The Plan

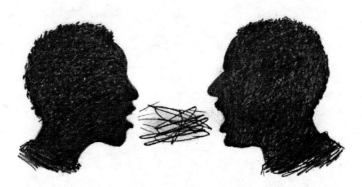

One day at the age of twelve I had come home from a fishing trip with my best friend's family. I saw this slender guy at my house. He said, "Hello, you must be Leon." I said, "Yea, but who in the hell are you?" He said, "My name is Mr. BH, I'm your mama's boyfriend." I said, "Oh really, my mamma don't need no boyfriend."

This guy was younger than any of the other boyfriends. He was loud all the time, but seemed to be a nice guy—at least when he was sober. BH had an alcohol problem and he was emotionally and physically abusive to my mother. On the weekends after drinking he would come home raising all kind of hell. He was also a Vietnam veteran so he would wake up in the middle of the night screaming. He and my mother would always get into arguments. He would curse, shout, and slam doors. He also hit my mother, but not in front of us.

By this time I had built up so much anger and resentment toward men that it had turned to rage. I plotted to murder Mr. BH. I told my brother the plan. One night Mr. BH and my mother started arguing in the front yard. I told my brother to go out the back of the apartment, along side of the house and on my signal go out and get Mr. BH's attention. Make sure his back is turned to me. I got a big butcher knife. The blade was about twelve inches long. As soon as Mr. BH's back was to me, I moved toward him ready to stab him from the back of his rib cage through his heart, hoping to kill him. But just as I was about to stab him I heard a gunshot. I looked around and there was my best friend's father standing with a shotgun in his hand. He had fired a shot in the air, because he saw what I was about to do.

Needless to say, Mr. BH ran away unharmed. This made me even more upset. My plan to kill this man had been destroyed by a gunshot. But looking back, that intervention was probably one of the kindest acts that anyone ever did on my behalf. I escaped becoming a criminal.

CHAPTER 4

Dreams, first hospitalization, Adolescent Unit

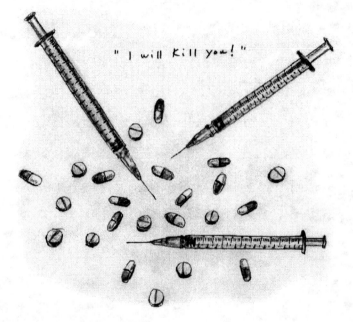

Though I never spent time in youth detention centers or jail, the anger, bitterness and hatred that filled my heart led me to be institutionalized at the age of thirteen. I had started the ninth grade. It was very exciting to go to high school. By this time the dancing group had faded away and I was focused on sports and my grades. I tried out for the ninth grade football team and made it. I started working out and making sure that I stayed in shape. Every day I looked forward to playing football. We had an outstanding ninth grade football team. I played running back and helped contribute to our winning season.

Then one night I had a dream. I dreamed that my mother had another seizure and this time she died in my arms. When I woke up from the dream it seemed so real to me that I actually thought my mom was dead. And I went to school that morning thinking that my mom had died. I was in a daze. When I arrived at school the women's basketball team was practicing and I lay down on the bleachers and fell asleep.

I remember my brother waking me up. He asked me what was wrong with me. He took me to the office and called my mother and said, "Hey, there's something wrong with Leon. You need to come to the school." My brother knew something was wrong because I was dressed like I didn't care about myself. This was not normal.

My mother came to the school and I'm still thinking in my head, in the dream, that my mother is dead. It didn't make sense. Since Mom was seeing a therapist and psychiatrist, she took me in to see them. They evaluated me and I told them that my mom died in my arms while having a seizure. I was crying and upset. I told them that since my mom was dead, I didn't want to live, that I couldn't live without my mom. I told them that I was going to kill myself.

The doctors made a decision to put me on some anti-depression medicine and sleeping pills, more than one thousand milligrams of medication. I went back to school a couple of days later and I was really out of it. I was heavily medicated. When I got home from school things got worse. I couldn't sleep. I was agitated and crying nonstop. So my mother took me back to the doctor and they decided to send me to the Georgia Mental Health Institute in Atlanta, Georgia.

I didn't know where I was going. My mother told me that I was going to a place where they would help me sort out my thoughts and deal with my anger, hatred and bitterness. So I agreed to go. After the hospital admission nurse and doctors evaluated me, they decided to admit me into the mental hospital. The hospital police officers came to escort us to the Adolescent Unit where I would stay. It didn't look like a hospital. It was a cottage.

I was tired and sleepy, emotionally exhausted, so I asked someone if I could lie down. They put me in a dark room with a mattress. Periodically, I asked them if I could go to the restroom. Eventually, they must have gotten tired of me asking, so one of the staff shut the door. I heard the lock click. I wondered why he locked the door. I thought, "I'm not a criminal."

Then I started knocking on the door trying to get the staff's attention. They pretended as if they didn't hear me. Then I started knocking on the door louder, calling for someone to unlock the door and let me out. I felt as if I was locked in jail, for no reason. I thought my family brought me to this place and they had me locked in this room. They left me. All I knew was that I didn't belong here.

I started screaming at the top of my lungs. I cursed. I banged on the door. Finally, a staff member came to the door and tried to calm me down. I screamed, "Why did you shut the door and lock me in this room." He said, "We did it for your safety so that you would not hurt yourself or anyone else." What did he mean? I didn't understand this. I was told that I was going to a place to get help and here I am locked in a room. I felt scared and angry. I continued to yell, curse and bang on the door.

Finally, a man and a woman looked through the small glass window of the door and asked me to step back. They opened the door. Then they charged at me. There were lots of them. It took about five to seven guards to subdue me. They took me down and a nurse gave me shots of medicine. Then they left and locked the door again. I didn't understand. I still kept shouting, cursing and banging on the door.

Then I saw my brother look at me through the glass window. I heard him tell them to let him come in and calm me down. I don't think my family understood why I was locked up either. When they opened the door to let my brother come in, I charged at him. I felt like nobody was on my side. I attacked my brother, filled with anger and hatred toward everybody, including him. Then the guards separated me from my brother, slammed the door and locked it, leaving me behind the door yelling, "I will kill all of you, if you don't let me out."

As my mom and brother were leaving me, I saw tears flowing from their eyes. I couldn't understand what was going on. I continued to raise hell and beat on the door until I got tired. Exhausted, I fell down on the mattress and went to sleep from being so tired and from the medication they had given me.

I woke to hearing a man's voice telling me it was time for me to go to my room. I had been in that observation room for two days. The man took me to my room. The staff person said, "Leon, this is your room." Here I am at the age of thirteen sitting in a mental institution but still not aware of where I was.

I remember the day after getting out of that dark observation room and into my own normal room. That night before I went to sleep I said a prayer. I prayed, "God, if you can hear me listen to me now. I don't know why I am here. My mother or brother, maybe they should be here instead of me." But I said, "May Your will be done."

I told God if he got me through this, then I would do His will.

I went to sleep that night and had another dream. In the dream I heard a voice say, "Leon, if you do my father's will I will be with you always to the very end of your life." The next day I came out of my room and started mingling with the other boys who were on the adolescent cottage. I carried my Bible with me. Though I didn't know the Bible, I felt compelled to carry it. But that feeling quickly died.

We had a unit meeting. I met the boys and girls who were staying at the cottage and I met the staff. The staff started going over the rules and regulations for those of us who were newbies. The staff member leading the meeting was Bob. He had long black hair and drove a Harley. All the kids were scared of him.

He went over the rules. He talked about cleaning rooms and the day area for both the boys and girls sides, obeying staff, times for breakfast, lunch and dinner, weekly school schedules. He explained the different levels that you can obtain. With each level came more responsibility. There were a total of three levels. At level three you had more freedom. You could go visit home on a pass, walk to the cafeteria with a staff member, go the basketball gym, and visit the store to purchase goodies.

This was my first meeting and I was already thinking that I needed to get to level three. It was not easy getting promoted through the levels. You had to prove yourself. My cottage housed adolescents from 13 through 17 years old. People were on this unit for all types of reasons. Some were court ordered because they had killed their parents. Some were waiting to go to juvenile detention because they had been in trouble with law enforcement. Some were gang members. Some were in foster care and waiting for foster families to take them in. For others this was their home because they didn't have a family on the outside. Still others were mentally challenged.

Mostly kids were there for a few months, then discharged. I became good friends with one patient. His name was Dan. Dan had a brain injury and he was in a wheel chair. He would sit in the day area playing games and having fun. Then all of a sudden, he would grab someone by the arm and become aggressive. Dan had two staff people assigned to him per shift. Whenever he became aggressive his staff would tell everyone to go to their room and they would take him down to the ground and restrain him. Then they would drag or carry him back to his room for lockdown. This was always a scary scene because you never knew if Dan was going to attack you. But sometimes I felt that I wanted to help him out of those restraints. He and I became the best of friends.

To me this place was like jail. The doors were locked all the time. The staff and guards were the only ones with keys to come in and out. There was a certain time to wake up. You would have breakfast, lunch and dinner together. My first visit at GMHI lasted six months. I saw a lot of kids come and go. I had a hard time when a kid was discharged, because I wanted to go home too. I thought to myself, "At least I have a home to go back to when I get out of here." Then I thought, "Why did my mother admit me to this place?"

The Adolescent Unit had paid staff to keep us kids straight. Doctors came in every morning to give physicals, medications and meet with patients. Teachers came during the week so we could go to school while we were there. Guards were called anytime one of us lost control or needed to be taken down. Restrained is what they called it.

I remember the first week the doctors started me on medication. I thought to myself, "Why do I have to take these pills? There's nothing wrong with me." But everyday at pill time the nurse would call my name and I would go up and get my medicine and take it. I hated taking this medication because it slowed me down. My speech became slurred and I gained a lot of weight. All I could think about was, "How can I play football taking all this medicine." I was not even concerned about my treatment plan. All I thought about was, "When can I get out of here?"

The teachers started to test me academically, to check my reading and math skills. Our school was in the basement of the cottage where we lived. We reported to school each day at 8:00 in the morning. We had a break from school and went to lunch, then back to school. Class was out at 3:00 in the afternoon. Then we had time to ourselves for the rest of the day. I would have a meeting with my therapist or psychiatrist once or twice per week. The therapy was not very helpful. All we talked about was how I was doing here. We never really dug deep into the issues that I had.

Every day was pretty much the same routine. On Saturdays we would have contests to see who had the cleanest room. I won this award several times. We would have cooking contests, dance contests, play football outside in front of the cottage, go to the gym on campus and play basketball, play pool, take field trips to the mall, museum, movies. The staff really tried to keep us active on Saturdays and Sundays.

After a month of being there I was promoted to Level 3. This meant that I could walk to the cafeteria by myself or with other kids on Level 2. I could go to the basketball gym without staff. I could go to the campus store to buy snacks. I could go home and visit my family on the weekends. But since I lived two hours away, I didn't make it home often, maybe once in the six months that I was there. It depressed me seeing other kids visit their family on the weekends or even being discharged.

I felt stuck in the cottage, not able to go home. This made me sad and even at times angry. During these moments I wouldn't follow the staff rules and regulations. I would get into fights with other kids. All they had to do was say the wrong thing to me and I would go off. This would land me back in the observation room, the cold, dark room with the mattress. Staff would put me in that room, close the door and lock it until I calmed down.

Many times it would be for a couple of days, depending on what I did or what staff was on duty. After six months in the Adolescent Unit I was released. Before I left the staff and kids threw me a big going home party. My mother, brother and neighbor friend came to pick me up. The party was awesome. I had a chance to show them some of my dance moves. Leaving there was bitter and sweet. Sweet, because I was going home. I felt as if I was being freed from jail. Bitter, because I had built some great relationships with female and male patients. I was doing well in school and I would miss everything about it. But I was ready to go. I vowed to myself, "I'm never coming back here again." I was ready to get back to my family and friends. I was a ninth grader in high school. I was ready to go.

CHAPTER 5

Back home, high school, meds and my return to GMHI

As we were traveling back home all I could think about was how glad I was to be free. My mother stopped at a gas station and she came back to the car with a Coke for me. She said, "Leon, it's time for you to take your medicine." I took it thinking, "I thought leaving the mental institution meant leaving the medicine behind too." But my mother made sure that I took my medicine every day. The medicine made me stiff, slow. I felt like a zombie.

I returned back home to my own bed and had a good night's sleep. The next morning I woke up and went to school. Everybody in school, especially those close to me, wanted to know where I had been. I didn't want to tell them that I had been admitted to a mental institution, so I lied and said I had been out of town visiting family. But they knew something was different about me. I was no longer the funny, loud class clown and athlete with whom everybody wanted to hang around.

The medication made me walk stiff. It slowed my speech and made me gain a lot of weight. Those closest to me knew something was wrong. Many of my friends stopped hanging with me. The girl that I was dating before I left broke up with me. She knew where I had been for the last six months and she said that I seemed so different when I returned. This made me feel sad, rejected, isolated and not wanted. Friends that I grew up with were now pushing me away. They didn't understand what I was going through, and, hell, I didn't understand it either. All I knew was that I was thirteen years old and having to take all this medication. It just didn't feel normal. None of my friends had to take medication. Everyone looked and acted normal, except me.

Here I was in the ninth grade, with hopes of playing football again. I was well known and liked by my peers, smart in school, with a bright future ahead of me. That is what I thought. I thought that being a teenager was the time when life was supposed to be great. This was the time in life when I was supposed to be trying to find myself, to fit in with my peers and have fun.

But I was feeling the opposite. Life was not fun. Friends were pulling away from me. I once had had a lot of girlfriends, but not now. The dancing group had dissolved. My home life was hard. Mom still had a live-in boyfriend that I didn't trust. My brother always played down my situation, saying, "There's nothing wrong with Leon." I felt so alone.

In the projects where I grew up I never felt that others hated me. They just didn't understand what I was going through. But I did have one close friend in the projects that I considered like a brother — Jermel. He and his family were there for me during these difficult times. His big brother would always have talks with me about focusing on football and getting ready for spring practice for the varsity team.

In the tenth grade I met a coach named Mike Cox, who coached the defensive backs. He took a special interest in me on and off the field. Coach Cox saw something in me that I didn't see in myself. He pushed me hard to excel in both the classroom and on the field. I started pouring myself into lifting weights and running. I was trying to get in shape. Training for football and playing football were like therapy for me. I could let out my anger and frustration on the football field by hitting someone real hard. It felt good. I loved the game for the contact. During football season I would take the medication that my mother would give me. But after the season was over, I would stop taking my medication.

Mom would give me the medication, but I would put it under my tongue and later spit it in the toilet. The reason I wouldn't take it was because it made me feel different. I didn't understand *why me*. I'm young, an athlete, healthy, cute, so why do I have to take this medication. So, for about three weeks I would spit it out when my mother gave it to me. Of course she didn't know it.

After a while I started not being able to sleep at night. My thoughts would begin to race at a hundred miles per hour. I became agitated and paced the floor a lot. It seemed like a motor was running in my ears and I could not stop it. I started sweating and crying uncontrollably. I wondered what was happening to me. Just three weeks ago I was okay. I realized that there where side effects to taking the medication, but it seemed to get worse the more I did *not* take it.

Once my mother discovered that I had not been taking my meds and she learned of the symptoms that I was having, she contacted the family psychiatrist. Without talking to me, the doctor quickly referred me back to the mental institution for the second time.

This time I did not willingly go. I didn't want to go back to that place. I fought, kicked and screamed all the way there. The police had to escort me back to the hospital and then eventually back to the adolescent cottage. The doctors gave me shots of medicine to calm me down. This time they did not put me in that isolation room.

Nevertheless, I was back at the place that I said that I would never come back to. This time my stay was for three months instead of six months like before. And this time the staff was all the same. They knew me. There were two patients there from the first time I was there, including one of my best friends, Daniel. The doctor's goal was to get me stabilized back on my medication. They changed the medication several times to try and get me on the right meds. Every time the nurse called for medicine time and gave me my medication, they would check under my tongue to make sure I swallowed it. I did take it and within three months I was stable on my meds.

They diagnosed me as bi-polar and discharged me. I went back home. But, since I never liked taking medication and didn't understand the importance of taking it, I stopped taking it periodically. I returned to the mental institution two more times.

THE TRANSFORMATION OF THOMAS WATSON

My senior year I was back at school and playing football. We had made it to the playoffs. My mother couldn't make it to the game because my grandmother was having triple bypass heart surgery. I had to make a hard decision to go see my grandmother in Virginia or stay back and play football. Since this was my last year and I had college scouts looking at me, I decided to stay and play football. We lost in that playoff game and that was my last game of the season.

The next week I stopped taking my medication. My mother was in Virginia taking care of her mother after the surgery. My brother and I were at the house. I was dating a young lady named Tiny. I wasn't my normal self. I became easily agitated, impatient. I got mad at Tiny without reason. I was losing control of my emotions and I became very angry.

One morning I woke up and could barely dress myself for school. I was shaking, sweating and pacing the floor. My mind was racing and I heard voices. I called Coach Cox and explained to him what was going on with me. He said that he would come over and pick me up for school. Coach got there and found me not looking like the normal Leon. He asked me what was wrong. He saw me sweating, shaking and pacing the floor. I told him that I was hearing voices. I finally dressed myself and got into his truck and went off to school. Coach told me that I looked like I needed some rest so he took me to the office in the basketball gym so I could get some rest there. I laid down and shut my eyes trying to get some sleep. But, every time I closed my eyes my mind would race faster and I would hear screaming voices.

I opened a door in the office, which led to the gym. I saw a janitor from a distance and I ran after him through the gym. The voices in my head told me to chase him, to hurt him. I chased him. When I caught him I started beating on him. Then other coaches and teachers came out from the teachers lounge and pulled me off of him. About five teachers took me into the teachers lounge. By this time I was trying to beat them too. I was worked up — out of control.

Someone went to get my best friend Jermel out of class. He came to the scene and called my name. All of a sudden I felt trapped, like I needed to get out of there, right now. Something inside me told me to jump out of this big window that was in the teachers lounge. So, when Jermel came near me I ran to the window and jumped out, cutting myself on the shoulder and arms. I landed on the cement below. Jermel and the teachers put me in a truck and took me to the football stadium until the paramedics arrived. The paramedics cleaned the blood off of me, stitched me up and took me to the local county hospital.

The doctor admitted me into the hospital. They really didn't know what was wrong with me because my mother was in Virginia and my brother couldn't be found. They had no clue that I was a bi-polar. And I was not about to tell them that I had stopped taking my meds. I stayed in the county hospital a week. Then my mom came home. They told her what happened at school. By this time I had become worse. I was agitated at the drop of a pin. Any noise would set me off. I thought my grandmother was dying and she was calling me on my hospital phone to tell me goodbye. I thought I was Jesus Christ and that I had certain powers. When my mother got to the hospital, she knew right away that I was not taking my medication.

The local police department took me from the county hospital back to the Georgia Mental Health Institute in Atlanta. It was a two-hour drive from my hometown. When we arrived they checked me in, just like the other three times before. Then the campus police officers escorted me to the Adolescent Unit for my fourth visit. All the staff that was there that night knew that I had stopped taking my medication. The experience this time was almost the same as the previous times. I knew the routine. I claimed the level rank quickly. I went to school.

This time they assigned a therapist to me — Patrice Thorpe. She met with me several times. We touched on some of my life issues, but we never dug too deep. She asked me why I didn't take my medication. I told her that I had been taking that medication since I was fourteen and I did not like the way it made me feel or look. I told her that none of my other friends where taking medication and I just did not think it was fair. She told me that it was important that I take it. I said okay, just so she would get off my back. I thought to myself, "She doesn't understand me. She doesn't have to live with this."

A few days later I was sitting in the lounge looking at TV. I saw my high school head football coach leaving the Adolescent Unit. I later found out that he came to meet with the doctors to see if I was able to play college football. There were schools interested in recruiting me. But I was not well enough to pursue playing football on the college level. This news made me so sad. I was devastated. I loved playing football and played it with a lot of passion. I went into a deep depression. My bi-polar condition and the medications were keeping me from going after my dream. This made me feel even worse about where I was in life at the age of seventeen.

CHAPTER 6

Patrice Tharpe, introduction to a new program CHRIS Kids

One day while I was still at the mental institution, my therapist Patrice Thorpe said to me that she never wanted me to come back here again. She told me of another place called CHARLEE, which is now CHRIS Kids, Inc. They had an independent living program. Patrice thought this would be a good program for me to branch out and live independently. I was discharged from the hospital and went back home.

When I returned back to school I learned that my school had changed from quarters to semesters. And since I had gone to school each time I was hospitalized, I had a lot of school credits, enough credits that I didn't have to take any classes my second semester in high school. So, I asked my graphic arts teacher if he would invest in me if I taught myself photography. He said yes. I taught myself black and white photography by going to the library and studying. My teacher had two cameras. I taught myself how to use a camera and the dark room. This was the start of the photography class at my school. I had photography class for about four hours and the rest of my day at school I had weight lifting and cooking class. I had to find classes to take that last semester. I graduated from high school in June 1987.

In December 1987, Patrice Thorpe called me from the hospital and asked my mom if I was still interested in the CHRIS Kids program in Atlanta, Georgia. My mother talked with me and I said yes. We received a call from someone at CHRIS Kids, who invited us to come to Atlanta for an interview and screening to see if they wanted to accept me or not.

My mother and I went to Atlanta for the interview. We met this lady named Kathy, the CEO of the organization. She explained to me that this is where kids from the age of seventeen to twenty-one, who are in transition from foster care, juvenile detention or a mental hospital can make their home while they learn to become self-sufficient adults. After leaving the interview we traveled back to Toccoa. I really didn't think they would choose me to come to the program.

So, when I got back home I started a job. Then I received a call from Miss Kathy saying that I was accepted into the program and she asked me if I wanted to accept. I took a couple of days to think it over carefully. Then I called back and told her yes.

CHAPTER 7

On my way, to where?

After packing my clothes in a big suitcase, I was on my way to the Amtrak train station heading for Atlanta and to CHRIS Kids' Independent Living Program. All I had was a suitcase and I remember thinking, "What am I doing, leaving the projects and my family." Then I remembered that this was my own decision, my choice. I made it myself and I was going to CHRIS Kids.

I left my hometown in Toccoa, Georgia to start my new life at CHRIS Kids on February 10, 1988. This was the best choice that I could have made because the next month my best friend Bobby, who I use to hang out with, went to prison for 20 years. There's no doubt that had I not made the decision to go to CHRIS Kids I would have been in prison with my best friend. I feared the unknown. I knew what to expect living at home, but going to Atlanta, I didn't know what to expect. As my mother took me to the Amtrak station I remember feeling excited and sad. I felt excited that I was going to a big city and sad that I was leaving my home. When the train arrived I gave my mother a kiss, then got on the train with my suitcase.

As I took the one-hour ride to Atlanta I sat at the window and started to daydream about my future. I thought to myself, "What am I going to do? Attend college, get a job...or what?"

CHAPTER 8

Independent living, party time, fighting the rules and a fifth hospitalization

The train arrived in Atlanta. I took a cab from the train station to

the CHRIS Kids office. There I met the residential counselor and

she packed my suitcase into her car and we were off to the place that I would be staying. We drove into an apartment complex and I was introduced to three other kids who were in the program. Then I was taken to my apartment. It was very nice, fully furnished including a telephone. I was introduced to my roommate. He was quiet but cool.

I remember thinking we have this big apartment to ourselves, "It's on now!" All I could think about was, "I'm in a big city, where are the parties, clubs and women?" The same day I crossed the street to go to the store and stopped this guy and asked him where the parties were. His name was Ed and he and I became best friends.

The next day all the residents met with the counselor. She started going over the rules and regulations. We had to look for a job and work 20-40 hours per week or be in school. Curfew was 11:00 pm on weekdays and 12:00 midnight on the weekends. We had to keep our apartment clean. We had to shop for our own groceries and cook for ourselves. I said to myself, "This is no group home. This is living on my own with a lot of rules and supervision." I had a social worker assigned to me. Her name was Jody. She took a personal interest in the development of all the kids. She did individual and group therapy sessions. Also, she taught us life skills: How to look for a job, interviewing skills and budgeting.

I started my first job working at a restaurant. I walked to work every day. After working there for six months, the manager said something to me that made me upset and I told him to step outside and we got to fighting. I hit him in the face. Then I got on top of him and starting hitting him in the face. The police came to the scene, but the manager didn't press charges against me. The officer let me go, but I was fired. I had moved to Atlanta to CHRIS Kids, but I brought all my anger, hatred, bitterness and fits of rage with me, and it came out on the job.

One night I came home to find my wallet missing from my apartment. I searched all over and couldn't find it. So, I suspected that my roommate had stolen my wallet and I confronted him. He said, "What if I did take it?" I went into his room and found my wallet, my ID and cards spread out on his bed. I literally lost it on him. I charged him, hit him in the face, stomped him with my boots. We must have fought for thirty minutes when the police came. After they pulled me off, I explained what happened. I didn't place charges against him, so they didn't arrest either of us. He remained my roommate, but we were never friends.

Ed was the guy that I became friends with. He was the first person that I met when I got to Atlanta. He was the one I asked about the clubs and parties. We walked to my apartment from the store. Then he told me that he was my neighbor. He was new in Atlanta too. We decided to go out to a club. At the first club we had to show identification. Ed was over twenty-one, but I was only seventeen, though I had a full mustache and looked older. But my identification would not allow me into most clubs. So that night was a waste, because in every club we went to, they checked my age. Ed told me not to worry. "Thomas," he said, "we'll fix this. Just come by my house tomorrow."

The next day I went to his house and met his father, Ed Sr. They had a photography business and made identification cards, passports, family photos at a flea market. So, my friend made me an identification showing that I was twenty-one years old. From this day on we hit the clubs hard. We partied six nights a week, sometime seven. We started out going to one club. Then that got boring so we found another club, until we had gone to every club in Atlanta. We were going to dance and pick up women. That was our mission.

I didn't hold to the curfew rules at CHRIS Kids. I came in after 1:00 or 2:00 in the morning. The resident counselor was asleep.

She didn't know that I was out that late. I didn't like curfews or rules anyway. I thought to myself, "I'm seventeen with my own place. Forget the rules and curfew." We would leave the clubs and our goal was for each of us to bring a lady home with us and we did. Ed would take his girl to his apartment and I would take my girl to my apartment. The lady would spend the night at my place, but we would get up early the next morning, and I would get her home before my resident counselor made her rounds to my place.

Many Saturday mornings Ed would knock on my apartment door, crying because he had caught an STD. I would have to drive him to the health department and sit there watching him take those pills. Ed could not swallow the big pills easily for some reason, so he cried taking them. We visited the health department for him five or six times over a year period. I never had to be treated for an STD.

One day I broke out with a bump on the back of my leg. Not a regular bump, it had a scab on it. But I didn't think twice about it until I started breaking out all over — on my arms and legs. I used to ride the public transit system and in the summer when it was 100 degrees, I wore long pants and a jacket to hide the sores. They would itch like crazy. I remember that I was scared that I had caught a serious disease from one of those girls. Once those scaly sores got on my face, I went to the county hospital. I was scared, I prayed to God, that I did not have AIDS. The doctors in the emergency room checked me out and broke the news to me. They told me I had a skin disease called psoriasis, that it was severe and I would need to be admitted into the hospital for at least one month for treatment. I was grateful that I did not have a sexual disease.

I was admitted to Grady Hospital on the dermatology floor. I underwent treatment three times a day for chronic psoriasis for one month. While I was in the hospital I met a young lady that I began to date. She was a nursing assistant. This was a relationship that I pursued after being discharged from Grady Hospital. The partying slowed down a lot. During this time I stopped taking my bi-polar medication. I thought that I was okay and didn't need the medication any longer.

Wrong. This lead me back to the mental hospital and this time I didn't return to the Adolescent Unit. I was admitted to the Adult Unit, which was very different. There were not a lot of activities for the adults. This stay was just a couple of weeks. The goal was to get me back on my medication and get me back to the CHRIS Kids program. The doctors got me stabilized back on my medication. Also, they tried to explain the importance of me staying on this medication because when I take the meds it works, but when I don't, I get sick. Here I was, an adult at eighteen and I still didn't understand the importance of staying on my medication. I went back to the CHRIS Kids program.

CHAPTER 9

Therapy, peeling the onion, independent living

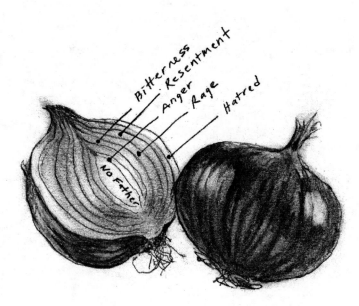

The CHRIS Kids social worker, Jody, referred me to a therapist at a local mental health center. I began therapy and seeing a psychiatrist for my medication on a regular basis. I would see the therapist every other week. Her name was Marsha. In the beginning I didn't want to see her or the doctor. I had to catch public transportation in order to make my appointments and I thought working was more important than keeping the appointments. But after a few good talks with Marsha, I decided to make my appointments a priority. Also, in order for me to remain in the CHRIS Kids program, they stipulated that I had to be in therapy. So I complied.

I remember my first session with Marsha. She tried getting to know me by asking me basic questions, but I was not very open or cooperative. After a couple of meetings I started to open up. I became more and more comfortable with Marsha and before long I was letting her into my world.

This was the first time that I ever had one-on-one counseling. In my previous hospitalizations I never had this. Counseling was always in a group. Marsha got to know me and I sensed that she really cared. Over the next few months I became more open about my childhood. I talked about how I felt when we left my dad behind in Virginia, how I felt growing up without a father. I talked about the many times I felt abandonment by men that I thought were going to be my father. I told her about my anger, bitterness and hatred. I told her what I had told no one. I told her about the time that I almost stabbed my mother's boyfriend. I told her about the hospitalizations, how the medications made me feel and the reason I did not like taking the medicine. I started to share more and more with Marsha.

It seemed like the peeling of an onion. The more I talked about these issues the more the peelings would fall off. As I sat there talking I felt relieved for the first time in my life. Just talking about how I felt through it all. This was therapy at work in my life at the age of eighteen. Marsha was able to explain to me why I was full of so much anger, bitterness, rage, hatred and resentment. It all stemmed from not having a father, but desperately wanting one. Marsha helped me see that I had a choice. I could choose to stay angry at the world for what I went through or I could take responsibility for my actions now.

It was *my* choice.

This was a reality check. Yes, I didn't have a father in my life. Yes, I was angry that I had spent so much time in mental hospitals, but this didn't' have to determine my future. I stopped and realized that I could still be in the hospital or in a youth detention center, but I wasn't. I was here working on me from the inside out.

Marsha introduced me to my doctor and I remember him asking me if I wanted to stay out of the hospital and I said yes. Then he explained to me the importance of taking my medicine and he explained that when I don't take it, I get sick. He gave me the example of the diabetic who needs insulin and if he doesn't take it, he will get sick. He told me that without my medicine I'm not balanced and will get sick and have to return back to the hospital. It finally clicked in my brain. I needed this medicine. Since then I've never stopped taking my medication, thanks to CHRIS Kids, Marsha and, of course, the choices that I made.

I still had some setbacks, however. After being at CHRIS Kids for two years I had found a job working for a welding company. I was being trained to be a mechanic. This was a great job with good pay. But I was fired from this job because of my anger. I got into a fight with a co-worker over words. I thought that I had my anger under control from the years of therapy with Marsha and CHRIS Kids. But I was still a work in progress. I still was going to therapy and trying to piece my life together. Therapy was working some. It helped me get in touch with why I was filled with anger and now I was learning, step by step, how to control it better.

CHAPTER 10

Meeting Juliana, church, God, finding my father, his death

One day while I was traveling home on the bus, this guy asked me if he could sit down beside me and I said, "No, it's too hot, I want to sit alone." Then he asked me again if he could sit down.

So I let him sit down. Later during the ride home he asked me what my name was and I looked at him like he was crazy, thinking, "Why is this guy asking me my name?" I refused to answer him or talk to him. Then he asked me what I was reading, so I told him that it was a book from my job. Next thing you know I'm telling him about the book that I'm reading and he listened. He invited me to a Bible study that he and some friends had at his home every Tuesday night. I wasn't interested. But he asked if we could exchange telephone numbers, so I gave him my number and he gave me his. As soon as I got off the bus I threw his number away and I forgot about him and the Bible study group. I was still living a wild life. Church and the Bible were the last things on my mind.

The very next Monday I received a call from the guy who had invited me to his Bible study. His name was Ray. I told Ray that I couldn't make it Tuesday because I had plans. The only plan I had was to party on Tuesday night. My friend Ed and I partied six nights a week. I told Ray that I couldn't make it, but I gave him permission to check back with me another time. I went on with my life.

Ray called me once a week for the next three weeks, until I became tired of him calling me. I went to the Bible study. When I stepped into his home I felt welcomed by everyone who was there. The Bible discussion topic was interesting. It got me thinking about God and my life. Though I was partying every night and having fun, I was empty on the inside. I was always searching for something to fulfill my life through partying, women or work. But, nothing seemed to fill the void that I felt.

After the first visit to Ray's Bible study he asked me if I wanted to study the Bible and learn about God. I said, "Sure." Growing up my mom had sent me to church and I thought I might be able to teach Ray and his friends something about the Bible, though I had never read it. I called my friend Ed and my girlfriend

Charlotte and told them that I would get together with them after 11:00 that night, instead of our regular time which was at 9:00. I didn't tell them the reason.

Ray, a few of his friends and I sat down for a Bible study and it was good. I agreed to get together again for another Bible study. I started reading the Bible more and more. I was learning about the Power of the Word of God, What a Christian is, and the Power of the Cross. Which meant that Jesus had died for me and all the inner pain that I had carried for years—the anger, bitterness, resentment, hatred and abandonment—could be healed by the blood that Jesus shed for me. I learned that I could be forgiven for all my sins and the hurts that I caused others. I also learned that I could forgive the people that hurt and abandoned me. Reading for myself about the life and death of Jesus helped me to forgive. I surrendered my life to God and asked him to take control.

I was baptized on March 26, 1989 and my life has never been the same since. I started going to Church with Ray. As I was studying the Bible, I started making changes in my life. I stopped partying, having sexual relationships, stopped drinking, cursing, fighting. My life changed because of the choices that I was making. Ed, my best friend, and Charlotte, thought I had lost my mind. They couldn't believe that I was not going to clubs with them anymore and that I had stopped cursing and sleeping with my girlfriend.

I asked both of them to come go to church with me. First they hesitated and said no. After a few months passed by and they saw that I was serious about my new life, they came to the Bible study group. They liked it too. Then they came with me to church. They liked church even more. We all liked church because you could come as you are, in jeans, tennis shoes, a suit or dress. It didn't matter. The word of God was being taught. You weren't being preached to, but taught. Both Ed and

Charlotte surrendered their life to God. We became soldiers for God. There are many people who also made the decision to follow Christ — just by seeing us change our lives.

My mother was still living in Toccoa, Georgia. But I would travel home and read the Bible with her and share with her how God's word had changed my life. She came to Atlanta to visit me at church and she surrendered her life to God. For the first time in our lives we were able to talk about my childhood and all that happened. She asked me to forgive her for exposing my brother and me to the different boyfriends she had had. She had no idea that was what caused a lot of my troubles. She asked me to forgive her and I did. We cried and forgave each other. She was not only my mother, she was now my sister in Christ. About a month later I moved my mother from Toccoa to Atlanta and we all were in the same ministry.

In 1990, I made a decision to leave CHRIS Kids and move in

with some of my church friends. This transition was challenging because I felt safe at CHRIS Kids and I had to step out of my comfort zone to build relationships with two new roommates. Being involved with this ministry helped me to trust people, especially men. Some of my best friendships were developed in this ministry. It wasn't easy but I worked on getting to know people. I still remained in therapy with Marsha for the next eight years. I developed convictions about taking my medication and this kept me out of the hospital.

In 1993, my mother told me about this young lady that she met. My mother told me that I needed to meet her because we had similar lives. I remember on a Wednesday night after church my mother introduced me to Juliana. She talked to me about the importance of me taking my medication and that she was taking medication for a mental illness too. I asked her what she wanted me to pray about for her and she gave me a couple of things to pray about. I called her up a couple of times to see how she was doing, but that was it. At that time I had no interest in her at all.

Later I found out that she thought I was cute and that she wanted to build a friendship with me. My focus was on the ministry and not on a girlfriend. I felt that my life was coming together. I had come to CHRIS Kids, started therapy, learned to work on me and surrendered my life to God. I was now active in ministry work, had developed great relationships, was working at AT&T and I was happy.

One day before Father's Day weekend I was sitting at my desk thinking about my father whom I didn't know. I called my mother and told her that I wanted to find my father for Father's Day. She told me that I had said to her as a kid, "One day when I grow up, I will find my father."

I asked my mother for my father's sister's last name and she told me Meade. I knew that he lived in the Charlotte, North Carolina

area. Since I worked for AT&T, I looked up every last name of
Meade in Charlotte and the surrounding areas. After calling the
first two names looking for my father with no success I almost
stopped. I decided to call one more person. A lady answered the
phone and I said, "Can I speak with Joshua Hazard?" The lady
said hold on and I heard her say "JP, pick up the phone." JP was
my father's nick name. My heart started pounding and I said to
myself, "What if this is him"? Then, I hung up the phone
because I didn't know what to say if it was my dad.

I called my mother back and said, "Guess what, Mom?" She
said, "You found your dad?" I said, "I think so, but I hung up."
Then my mom gave me a pep talk, saying, "Thomas, you always
said when you grow up, if your father is not dead, you were
going to find him and every Father's Day you always ask me
about your dad." She told me to pray and call him back. So I did
pray. Then I called back. The phone rang and a man answered
the phone. I said, "May I speak with Joshua Paris Hazard?" And

the man said, "This is he." Then I said, "This is Thomas Leon Watson, your son." There seemed to be silence on the line for at least ten minutes. Then I said, "Whatever happened in the past is in the past. I forgive you." He said, "Thank you, son." That helped break the ice. We had our first talk in twenty-five years. He was very glad to hear from me.

After talking with my dad, I made plans to visit him in Kannapolis, North Carolina, where he lived with his nephew. He told me that he had both of his legs amputated, which I already knew about from the last time he spoke with my mother. I called my mother back and told her the news and I started telling my co-workers and friends. Then, I made plans to visit him that weekend for Father's Day.

My friend Dushun and I traveled from Atlanta to Kannapolis to visit my dad. I remember that my mother told me how much I looked like him, but I wondered how I could look like my father when I looked just like my mother. We drove up to the house and I was nervous about meeting my dad. We went into the house and I met him. We hugged and began to talk. We had a lot of catching up in one weekend. And I met a lot of relatives.

That Saturday morning I picked him up and we went to Shoney's for breakfast. We talked for hours. I learned that my dad was six feet seven inches, played high school and college basketball and football. I also learned that we liked and disliked some of the same foods, we loved to eat, and we liked sleeping on a cold floor. His family loved him and I *did* look like my father. I was having such a great time that I didn't want to go back to Atlanta. It was great meeting my father. He answered a lot of questions that I had. We talked a lot over two days. And I knew that I would return soon.

On the way home I told Dushun that I could see myself moving to Charlotte to be closer to my father, especially since we had a sister church in Charlotte and I had met some members of their congregation. I figured that I could come and live with some of the brothers in the church. But this was just a thought. My dad and I stayed in touch. I started praying about moving to Charlotte and I made more visits to see my dad and visit the church.

Then, I started talking to my employer AT&T about transferring me to the Charlotte office. Everything came together so I was planning my move to Charlotte. The date for me to leave was set. I hated leaving all my family and friends in Atlanta, but this was a chance for me to get to know my father better. My friends gave me a big going away party.

Before leaving for North Carolina, I asked Juliana, the young lady that I met a year ago, out for a date. We went to underground Atlanta and lunch. The conversation was great. We shared our lives with each other. She even told me that she liked me. I told her that I was not looking for a relationship because the next day I would be moving to North Carolina. We still had an awesome date, but my heart and mind were in North Carolina.

I had a bag filled with emotions and feelings. One minute I was happy about moving, the next minute I was sad. I had a strong support system around me with my mother, friends, therapist and the church. Now I was going to a new town, family, friends, job and church. This would be a lot of pressure for anybody. But for me, a twenty-five year old with a bi-polar mental illness, I knew it was major change.

When I first got there I did well. I told my new roommates about the medication that I was taking and about my history. I was getting settled in at my new job. Juliana would call me at work and we would talk. She told me that she was praying that I would return back to Atlanta. I told her that was not going to happen any time soon. Then I ran out of medication and I had not yet established a relationship with a doctor to get my medicine.

After being out of my medication for three weeks, I started to get sick mentally.

I felt it coming. So I got a Greyhound bus back to Atlanta and stayed with some friends over the weekend until I could visit my doctor on Monday morning. But during the weekend I got worse. I couldn't sleep. My thoughts were racing. I became paranoid thinking that someone was after me. I started hearing voices. I left the house on a winter night without a shirt and took public transportation to my mom's house. She opened the door and immediately knew that I was having a bi-polar episode.

Some of my friends picked me up from my mom's house and took me to a county hospital. But they would not see me without insurance. Monday morning my friend Tom took me in to see my therapist Marsha. They sent me back to the Georgia Mental Health Institute. This time the doctors and staff knew me. They knew this was my fifth time being there. The doctors explained to me that if I could only understand the importance of staying on this medication that I would never have to come back there. Someone explained, once again, that I was like a diabetic that needs his insulin. They explained that my medicine is like insulin, that I need it to be healthy mentally. After ten long years, it all made sense.

I remember in the summer of 1994 I made a decision in that hospital to always take my medication. I would stay out of the hospital and lead a productive life. I'm happy to say this is 2013 and I've not been hospitalized since 1994. That's been seventeen years and I'm still faithfully taking my medication today. I understand that I need it.

Shortly after getting out of the hospital I went on my second date with Juliana. It was a terrible date. I tried opening her car door and she wouldn't allow me to. I took her to a nice restaurant and she wanted to eat somewhere else. It was a bad date. I told some friends that she was not the one for me. I started pursuing other women. Also, I was still focused on my newfound relationship with my father. I was in contact with him daily by phone. My father and his family really never understood why my move to North Carolina was cut so short. He knew that I was in the hospital but I never went into the details of my bi-polar illness.

Then a couple of months later I received at call at 12:00 midnight that my father had died. He died in March 1995. This news brought a lot of sadness and many tears. But I was glad that I had met him a year earlier and that we had good quality time with each other before he passed. Later I found out that before I had contacted my father, he had lost the desire to live. He had stopped eating, coming out of his room, shaving or caring for himself. He was down and out. When I suddenly came into his life, it changed his perspective. He started eating again and socializing. He got a clean shave, because I had found him and was coming to visit.

Finding my father gave him something to live for and it helped me to be a better man too. I was able to forgive him for not being there for me. I was able to forgive all the men my mother dated, who never stayed around. I was able to trust and love people, men or women, for the first time in my life. Basically, I was able to heal from the emotional abandonment that I felt. Spending time with my dad changed my life forever. I am eternally grateful that I had the chance to meet him before he died.

CHAPTER 11

Marrying Juliana, a wedding from heaven, my mother's death

I went on my third date with Juliana. It was a better date than the previous one. She allowed me to open her doors, pick the restaurant and we had a great time. We talked a lot. After this date we kept in touch with each other. We talked on the phone and in fellowship at church. Our conversation was always spiritual. Juliana and I became best friends and we had a lot in common. The more we got to know each other the more I began to like her.

Before meeting Juliana I had prayed that the next woman I dated would become my wife and would have the following qualities. Openness. I prayed that she would be real and open about her life and that I would not have to pry out information. Laughter. She would love to laugh and have a good time. Athletic. She would love sports and like watching sports with me. Love for God. She would love God more than me. Lastly, she would have a love for kids. As I got to know Juliana, she had all of these qualities and more. I started liking her so much that I decided that I wanted to date her exclusively. I told her that I liked her and instead of her embracing the idea she ran away from me. When I told her that I liked her she said that she did not like me and feelings were not mutual.

Later, she explained the reason she ran was because she was afraid to give her heart in a committed relationship. After a few days passed she came to her senses and confessed to me that she liked me too. I knew that she liked me. So, February 14, 1995, I asked her to be my girlfriend and to promise that we date only each other. She said yes and this started our two years and ten months of dating. During this time I would write her love letters and mail them Federal Express, addressed to her. I also gave her a lot of flowers and tried my best to be romantic. My mother liked Juliana a lot. And she also loved our decision to be a dating couple.

The longer we dated the more we learned about each other. I told her about me, my childhood, my being bi-polar, taking medication, five hospitalizations, about my dad. Juliana knew everything about me. I learned about her childhood, that she was schizophrenic and took medication too. Two peas in the pod! We would remind each other to take our medication. She was different from any other woman that I had dated because she accepted me for who I was. The more she learned about me the more she loved me. I treated her like a queen and she treated me like a king without needing to have sex. Our relationship was totally platonic for two years and ten months. This was hard but it was worth the wait.

On December 20, 1997, I took Juliana on a date to the Sundial restaurant at the Westin Peachtree Plaza in downtown Atlanta. Her twin sister and her husband were on this date with us. We had a nice dinner and danced at the restaurant. Then we went on a horse carriage ride around downtown. Halfway through the ride, I presented Juliana with an early Christmas gift. It was a big box wrapped in gold paper. She opened the box and found a photo album filled with every card and letter that I had given to her. Her roommate had gotten these for me. I had her tell me what each card meant as we rode in the carriage. My brother-in-law was recording the entire night.

Then I broke out with a poem called *I Believe You Can Fly*, but I changed the title to *Fly Together Forever*. As I was reciting the poem, I fell to one knee, pulled out the ring and asked her to marry me. She couldn't believe that I was proposing to her. First, she became silent, then her eyes got big and she started screaming and saying, "Yes, Yes." She started jumping up and down, almost forgetting about the ring. Then, I put the ring on her finger and gave her a kiss.

I had planned a surprise engagement party and all of our friends were there to encourage us on this big night. The next six months were spent planning the wedding. This was a wedding from God. We had no idea how this wedding would be paid for. But, it all happened. Juliana's friend took her shopping for her wedding dress and paid for it. A friend of mine paid for the cake and the wedding pictures.

On June 13, 1998, we were married. There were four hundred

guests at our wedding. I remember when the door opened and I saw Juliana standing there looking so beautiful. The aisle that she was walking down was so long, I met her in the middle of the isle on one knee. Then we walked down the aisle together to the preacher and he married us. This was the happiest day of our lives, being together.

Then two years later Juliana became pregnant. We were all excited that Juliana was pregnant, especially my mother. She was looking forward to being a grandmother. But, two months later Juliana lost the baby. Then six months later, I found my mom dead. She died from a heart attack in her sleep on Friday, October 13, 2000. This was the darkest day of my life. Her death was unexpected. In her will, she indicated that she wanted me to do her eulogy. God gave me the strength and courage to do this. Her death brought my brother and me closer together. But losing my mother was a big deal. Thank God for my wife and the support system that I had. I have great memories of my mother that help me get through the difficult days. I thank God for the time we had together and she will never be forgotten.

CHAPTER 12

Connecting with Kathy, volunteering at CHRIS Kids, being a spokesperson

I spent the next five years working in corporate America and learning how to be married. We had our share of good times and bad times. Then early in 2005, I reached out to Kathy Colbenson, the CEO of CHRIS Kids, to let her know how I was doing and to say thank you for having such an impact on my life. Needless to say, she was very delighted to hear from me. We got together for lunch and she asked me about my life since CHRIS Kids. I shared with her how I had made some spiritual decisions to follow God and how I had a strong support system in the church, that I was married to a wonderful women and I had been working in corporate America for many years.

I also shared with her how I had conquered my anger and was now living a productive life in society. Kathy sat there with the biggest smile on her face and tears in her eyes. She told me that I had beaten the odds. I was not a statistic that ended up in jail or dead. She was so proud that I had found God, a loving wife and a stable career. I expressed my gratitude to her for giving me the opportunity to be accepted into the CHRIS Kids program in 1998. I expressed to her that the one decision that changed the course of my life was coming to CHRIS Kids. I reminded her of all the counseling, conversations about me taking my medication, that it all paid off.

Before leaving the restaurant I told Kathy that I wanted to get involved with CHRIS Kids. I wanted to volunteer my time and give back to the organization that helped save my life. So she invited me the CHRIS Kids Annual Achievement Luncheon for the kids. This is where the kids are recognized for their personal achievements in school and in CHRIS Kids. I had the opportunity to meet the kids and share a good lunch.

As I sat there listening to the guest speaker talk to the kids, my heart was burning with desire to share something with the kids. I told Kathy's assistant that I wanted to speak. I didn't know what they would say because they were following a program and I wasn't on it. They said okay.

So Kathy introduced me to the kids and the audience. She said, "We have a special guest in the room today. This young man was in the CHRIS Kids program seventeen years ago and he is a success story."

I stood up and shared my story with the kids. It seemed that every kid's eyes and attention were on me. They wanted to hear what I had to say. I told my story and about my time at CHRIS Kids. I congratulated them on their achievements and inspired them by sharing the struggles that I had and that I had overcome. The kids were very receptive. I spoke with many kids afterward who thanked me for sharing. Many of CHRIS Kids corporate donors told me afterward they were inspired and could see the success of CHRIS Kids through my life.

This was the first time I shad spoken to a crowd of people about my story, but it felt good and right. I felt like this was what I was created to do. There were other opportunities that came up for me to share my story. The next time was a corporate event at General Electric, where there were about two hundred employees. Kathy introduced CHRIS Kids and I shared my story of how the organization helped me. Again, this felt very natural for me to share my story and the company paid me my first check for speaking. I was excited. One hundred dollars for ten minutes. I liked this. I said to myself, "I can do this for a living!"

I started doing some volunteer work with the kids. My wife and I met the older kids, age seventeen to twenty one, and taught them about finances. We met every other Tuesday at CHRIS Kids' home office. We taught them budgeting skills, about credit and interviewing. I enjoyed this, but I found that I had a passion for telling my story.

In October of 2005, Kathy asked me if I would be the keynote speaker at the Annual CHRIStal Ball event, which is their major fundraising event for the year. I accepted this invitation. What I did not know was that I was going to be one of the recipients of the CHRIStal Ball Visionary Award, given to two people for their involvement with the organization. I received a Tiffany's Watch and Tiffany's Crystal Plate, engraved with the Visionary

Award comments. Then after all this I had to deliver the keynote speech. This was the first time I ever spoke to a crowd of more than four hundred people. I shared my story and it was received with great applause.

I continued with volunteer work at CHRIS Kids. In 2009, Kathy asked me to become a board member. She presented the idea to the board of directors and they accepted me. I grew up as a CHRIS Kid, but now I found myself sitting on the board as a board member, learning how the organization is run from the inside. I am very impressed with the leadership of this organization and how it has thrived, even during a down economy. This organization raised more than $12.1 million for a Capitol Campaign, which helped complete the Graham Circle Project, a permanent supportive housing development for 17 – 24-year-old, single or parenting, youth who are aging out of foster care, or who are homeless.

My story is ongoing, but I will always be a CHRIS Kid. Being a client, a board member, and now a mentor has changed my life and I am forever thankful.

And today, I am paying it forward.

Sometimes a Simple Idea Can Change the World

A History of CHRIS Kids

CHRIS Kids started as a simple idea. The idea that kids who bounce around from place-to-place in foster care may need something more than their current foster homes were providing. These kids had major behavioral and mental health challenges resulting from years of abuse and neglect. They were victims of trauma – and were further traumatized with every move. They did not belong in hospitals or institutions. Instead, maybe these kids needed to live in loving homes, in local neighborhoods and have more specialized support that recognized and understood their traumas. Maybe these kids needed therapy, counseling and other clinical services to address their core issues. This idea started what is now CHRIS Kids.

From its founding to today, CHRIS Kids has evolved and responded—just like the kids the organization has been helping. Core values continue to be defined by the CHRIS name: **C**reativity, **H**onor, **R**espect, **I**ntegrity, **S**afety. The mission grew to include strengthening families in the hope of helping kids safely remain in their own homes, preventing the disconnections and repeated traumas of moving from foster home to foster home. Each decade brought new and deeper understandings, adaptations, programs, facilities and services, while the mission to heal children, strengthen families and build community has remained constant.

In 1981, the Junior League of Atlanta, in collaboration with the Menninger Foundation, decided to do something to help these children. Together, they established Georgia CHARLEE (Children Have All Rights—Legal, Educational, Emotional) to serve severely emotionally troubled, abused and neglected foster children.

The organization was the first of its kind in Georgia and was renamed CHRIS Kids in the ensuing years. It began with three group homes for six children in three different neighborhoods. The goal was to provide a "family-like" atmosphere for kids, ages 6-17, where they could learn (by doing) how to live successfully in a "family" in the community. Originally the group homes had both boys and girls and a mix of ages, although most of the kids in the program today are teenagers.

This program operates like most "mainstream family homes" in that meals are prepared together, homework is completed, chores are required and each kid can participate in after school or recreational activities that suit their interests. The kids go to public schools and are often enrolled in Special Education classes. They receive mental health therapy, counseling and a large dose of adult support and guidance. This program has grown to include eight group homes in five different metro Atlanta counties and is called JourneyZ to represent the "journey" these kids are making to become productive adults.

In 1986, CHRIS Kids recognized that a significant number of teenagers in foster care were "aging out." This means that the teens were turning 18 and becoming "adults," but with nowhere to turn. Many of these youth became homeless because they had no family, no support systems and did not have the independent living skills to survive on their own. CHRIS Kids stepped up to fill the gap. This new program, another first of its kind, focused on youth transitioning out of foster care. It operated in two-bedroom apartments for youth, ages 17-21, so that they could learn life skills and receive mental health treatment, therapy and counseling services. The program focused on the tangible outcomes of obtaining a high school diploma, finishing a GED, getting a job, going to college or joining the military.

Now, 32 years later, this successful program includes homeless youth with special outreach to lesbian, gay, bisexual and transgender youth who are disproportionately homeless, as well as the original target group of youth aging out of foster care. The program is called TransitionZ and is offered in a supportive housing apartment complex named Summit Trail Apartments. TransitionZ at Summit Trail represents the "transition" from child to adult and the challenge, hard work and dedication it takes to reach the summit of self-sufficiency.

CHRIS Kids gained attention statewide due to its strength based and family focused work, its ability to provide services effectively within the community as well as in a family's home, and because of its clear understanding of the impact of trauma. Responding to gaps in Georgia services, the organization stepped forward to create innovative pilot initiatives for a children's shelter with special assessments and for a summer camp for kids who could not attend mainstream summer camps. And in the late 1990s CHRIS Kids created the first community based wraparound pilot for the State of Georgia.

In 2007, CHRIS Kids addressed the need for affordable, sometimes free, high quality behavioral health services. This led to the opening of the CHRIS Counseling Center for the community at large. With the center's opening, the organization was able to further promote an emphasis on understanding trauma and providing trauma informed care. Reducing and eliminating barriers to service, CHRIS Kids leveraged its innovative ability. Through high fidelity wraparound, CHRIS Kids provided care coordination for youth who qualified for psychiatric hospitalization, and the program demonstrated that with the right approaches, children can safely stay in their own homes and out of hospitals at great cost savings.

In addition, CHRIS Kids' Education and Training initiatives offer internships and help promote creative, best practice approaches; educate and prevent child abuse, particularly child sexual abuse; and help build a strong child welfare and clinical workforce on behalf of those served.

Today, CHRIS Kids' Family of Services and collaborative partnerships continue to fill gaps and introduce new approaches. CHRIS Kids has a proven track record of innovation, leading change in the community and has won numerous recognitions and awards for excellence in both service and management. The mission remains steady: to heal children, strengthen families and build community.

CHRIS Kids has transformed more than 20,000 lives. The kids who come to CHRIS Kids are often on the path to a bad outcome. The families served are among the most challenged.

But at CHRIS Kids — belief turns into action, ideas into realities and potential into success. While programs and services have adapted to societal needs, the mission has not. Thanks to the support of staff, volunteers, donors and partners, CHRIS Kids has grown to include an integrated Family of Services designed to give children and families a hand up, not a hand out, so that they can realize their potential for self sufficiency and good citizenship. The goal is always to discover and unlock the potential that slumbers in each child, in each family, in each volunteer, in each donor and in each employee.

About the Author

Thomas Watson lives and works in Atlanta, Georgia. He serves on the Board of CHRIS Kids and is currently pursuing a B.S. degree in Business Administration, specializing in Management & Leadership at South University. To schedule a speaking engagement, visit his website www.tlwtransformation.com.

As a professional clinical therapist working with child, adolescent and adults and close friend and brother for eternity of Thomas Watson, I recommend this book to all professionals, parents and, especially, young individuals who seek to understand life and the world of mental health through the personal and individualized eyes of a young man and his own past struggles with his mental health and self acceptance. This book is a very powerful read for all teens and adults, regardless of race and personal background.

Jermel Dortch, BA, ACT, CAMC of Glorious Beginning, LLC

There probably isn't a day that goes by when one doesn't hear negative information about the plight of young African American males. I met Thomas in 1994 and this book characterizes a young man who has exemplified perseverance, selflessness, and unconditional forgiveness. This book is rich with insights that will inspire young men to dream even if they have had to deal with trying situations. All who read this book and take the journey with Thomas will be moved to believe in the everlasting hope of change and transformation.

Dr. Burrell Theopolis Pope, III

As a pastor and coach, I am always seeking to believe that personal and community transformation is possible. I have known Thomas for almost two decades, and he is the 'real deal' – a gift to all of us. The story that my good friend Thomas Watson outlines in this book will inform, inspire, encourage and enable any sincere reader to appreciate the potential inherent in all human beings.

Dr. Benjamin U. Barnett, Pastor

I am very close to this young man and his situation. I know first hand what he has gone through especially in his teenage years. Having had the privilege of working with him in football at Stephens County High School makes this story even more special for me. After reading his book it makes me so very proud of him and the way in which he has overcome his illness. Thomas's story is a rock for all who are in the same situation. The one element that is most impressive is his faith in God and willingness to follow in that path.

Coach Mike Cox, Stephens County High School